A You Can Make It Book

You Can Make It:

Hope on The Journey of Motherhood

All rights reserved. No part of this book may be reproduced or transmitted in any form or by any means without written permission from the author.

All Scripture quotations, unless otherwise indicated, are taken from the Holy Bible, New International Version®, NIV®. Copyright ©1973, 1978, 1984, 2011 by Biblica, Inc.® Used by permission of Zondervan. All rights reserved worldwide. www.zondervan.com The "NIV" and "New International Version" are trademarks registered in the United States Patent and Trademark Office by Biblica, Inc.®

Scripture quotations marked (AMP) are taken from the Amplified Bible, Copyright © 1954, 1958, 1962, 1964, 1965, 1987 by The Lockman Foundation. Used by permission.

Scripture quotations marked (GNT) are from the Good News Translation in Today's English Version- Second Edition Copyright © 1992 by American Bible Society. Used by Permission.

One Scripture is noted from The Authorized (King James) Version. Rights in the Authorized Version in the United Kingdom are vested in the Crown. Reproduced by permission of the Crown's patentee, Cambridge University Press

"Scripture quotations are from the ESV® Bible (The Holy Bible, English Standard Version®), copyright © 2001 by Crossway, a publishing ministry of Good News Publishers. Used by permission. All rights reserved."

Scripture quotations marked (NLT) are taken from the Holy Bible, New Living Translation, copyright ©1996, 2004, 2015 by Tyndale House Foundation. Used by permission of Tyndale House Publishers, Carol Stream, Illinois 60188. All rights reserved.
You Can Make It: Hope on the Journey of Motherhood
Copyright © 2021 by Leticia M. Starks-Underwood
Published By: You Can Make It Books, LLC
www.youcanmakeitbooks.com

ISBN: 978-1-7366651-8-3

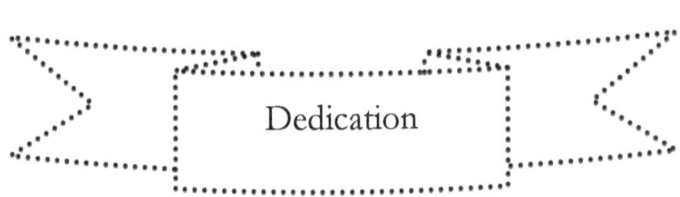

# Dedication

This book is dedicated to all the mothers and mothers-to-be. You rock!

Proverbs 31:25 (NLT)

"She is clothed with strength and dignity, and she laughs without fear of the future."

## Table of Content

Acknowledgments..............................................7

Introduction......................................................10

GOD Makes No Mistakes..............................19

Your Baby Feels What You Feels...................27

His Love Makes Me Beautiful!....................... 34

You're Not Failing; You're Learning................40

GOD'S Gift of Mothering-Grace.....................47

Time Heals All Wounds ................................55

Full, Yet Running Off Empty ........................62

Hope in GOD'S Promises............................69

Short Affirmations ...................….......…….77

Personal Affirmation ...............................78

Bible Verses ..........................................79

Journal For Weary Days ..............…............84

My Story ...............…...........................88

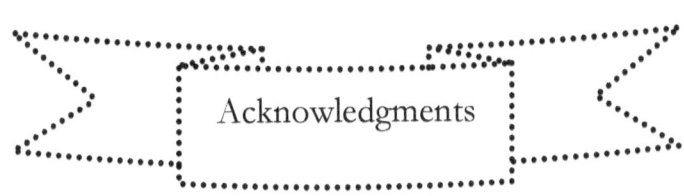

# Acknowledgments

I would like to acknowledge my Heavenly Father, who is my creator and sustainer.

I would like to acknowledge my Husband, children, parents, grandparents, and bonus parents.

I would like to acknowledge all those who have played a tremendous role in helping the You Can Make It Books Series, from the editor to each writer that contributed their testimony.

When children are born, they have no awareness of limitations! They must be lied to and convinced that they are not POSSIBLE!

Oscar J. Nelson Dowdell-Underwood, Ph.D

*The Father of Possibleology and Possibility Education*

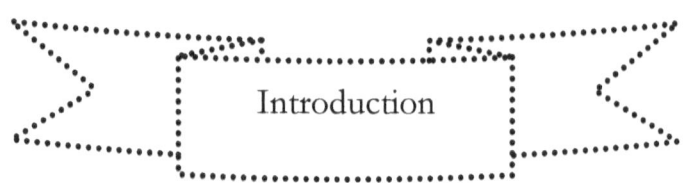

## Introduction

"You're pregnant!" While many women exclaim at the announcement of this news, for others, these words create a longing for the same. Pregnancy is a wonderful thing, and babies are a gift from GOD. Whether babies come into this world planned or by surprise, they are here for a purpose. Our jobs as mothers are to protect and nurture our children so that they can fulfill the plan and purpose of GOD. However, that journey can become weary.

As mothers, we wonder if we are a good parent. We question if we are giving our children the best life. We struggle with who we are as mothers. We wonder if we will ever return to who we were before having children. There's a cost to being a mother, but a well-deserving cost.

It is easy to become discouraged or sometimes think we are in this all alone. GOD wants us to depend on Him and not try to do everything on our own. The Bible says when we are weak; in actuality, we are strong in Him (2 Cor. 2:10). GOD wants to help us.

*You Can Make It: Hope on The Journey of Moetherhood* is written to empower and strengthen mothers and mothers-to-be. We all have our own story and struggles as a mother. However, it is crucial that as you journey through life as a mother or a mother-to-be, you understand that you're not alone. Not only do you have other moms cheering you on, but most importantly, you have GOD rooting for you.

This book is comprised of testimonies from different moms sharing their stories, short prayers, affirmations, and Bible verses to empower and encourage you. I pray as you read this book that you will find the strength to be encouraged, empowered and to fight the everyday worries and challenges of motherhood. I pray that as a mom, you find the drive to keep pursuing your dreams and trusting GOD while parenting your children. The Bible says that GOD will never put more on us than we can bear, including in our personal lives.

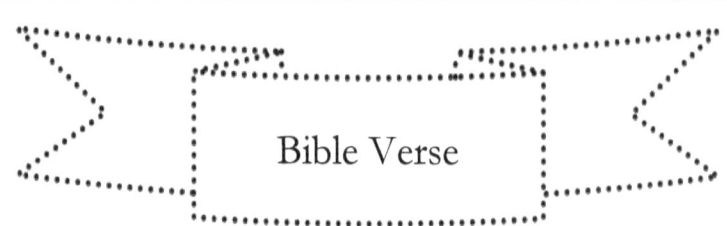

Bible Verse

"Stand firm in the faith; be courageous; be strong"

~ 1 Corinthians 16:13

# Prayer Over My Pregnancy

## Prayer Over My Child

## Prayer Over My Life

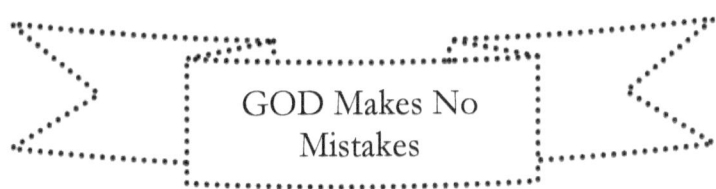

# GOD Makes No Mistakes

GOD makes no mistake! By default, His deity prevents it. However, we make mistakes. As Christians, according to Romans 8:28, "And we know that in all things God works for the good of those who love him, who[a] have been called according to his purpose." Therefore, when children are brought into this world, they are not mistakes; they are gifts from GOD. The timing may be off for some and perfect for others; while some have waited multiple seasons to bear a child, the gift is intentional. However, or whenever a child comes into this world, they are here for a purpose. So, never think that your child or children are a mistake.

They have a purpose, and so do you. Although they come and shake up and rearrange our lives, they are a gift from GOD. My children are one of the greatest gifts I could have received from GOD. However, with my second child, I didn't understand GOD'S plan when I found out I was pregnant. GOD had to remind me of His plan for my son, and that plan is for him to carry out the name of His Great Grandfather. As much as I battled with the thought of being pregnant, I had to realize that all things work together for those who love Him and are called according to His purpose. The hope, joy, and possibilities that my son has brought to our family since his birth, I wouldn't and couldn't change it for the world. I never thought or said he was a mistake; I just couldn't fathom the thought of being pregnant and during the Covid-19 pandemic. One principle I will always hold firm to that my grandfather and pastor always says is, "If GOD allowed it, it must serve a purpose." I might not have known at the time I found out I was pregnant the magnitude of GOD'S purpose for my son's existence. Truthfully, I still don't know the depth of it, but what I do know is that he's here on an assignment for GOD, and so is my daughter.

So, GOD makes no mistakes. It's not in His DNA. However, our plans may not be His plans. I never thought that I would get pregnant in 2020, but it was GOD'S plan and purpose for my life. In fulfilling His plan for our lives, He will never put more on us than we can bear (1 Cor. 10:13). GOD will give us the strength to be a GODly mother to protect and nurture our children. Paul wrote in 2 Corinthians 12:10 That when we are weak, we are strong in Christ: "That's why I take pleasure in my weaknesses, and in the insults, hardships, persecutions, and troubles that I suffer for Christ. For when I am weak, then I am strong" (NLT). So, when you feel weak as a mother, it is imperative to turn to GOD to receive the strength and Grace to travel on this journey called life.

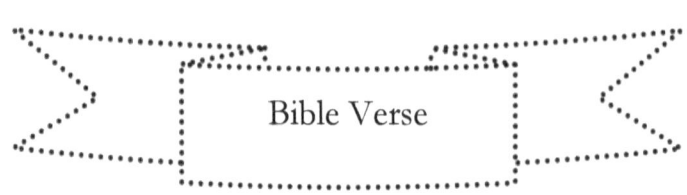
Bible Verse

"That's why I take pleasure in my weaknesses, and in the insults, hardships, persecutions, and troubles that I suffer for Christ. For when I am weak, then I am strong" (NLT).

~ 2 Corinthians 2:10

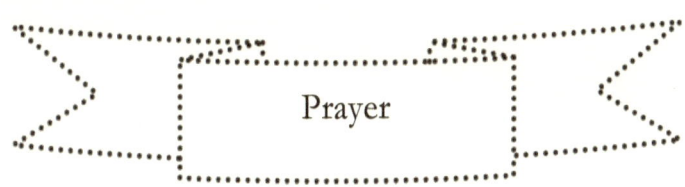

# Prayer

Abba, Father. My Heavenly Father, I thank you for my child(ren). They are a gift from you to me. For your Word says, "Children are a gift from the Lord; they are a reward from him" (Psalms 127:3). Since my children are a gift from you, I will cherish and protect them. I am blessed to have my children, and my children are blessed to have me. My children are not a mistake. My children are here for a purpose, and GOD, I ask for the Grace to guide them into the very purpose you created them to do. I don't want to hinder my children's purpose. In all that I do, I ask for the Grace to be a GODLY example to them.

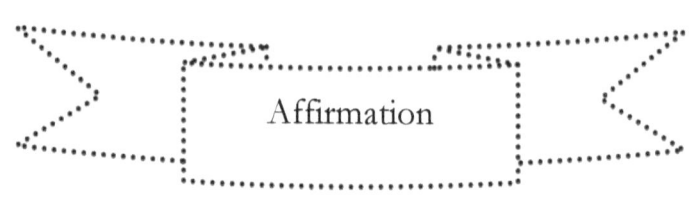

## Affirmation

My children are a precious gift from GOD.

They are here on an assignment to do GOD'S Will and not my will.

GOD makes no mistakes or accidents, and that includes my children.

He's an intentional GOD, and my children are here for a great purpose.

When GOD chose to create you in His Image, He also chose to create you as POSSIBLE in every area of your life.


~Oscar J. Nelson Dowdell-Underwood, Ph.D

*The Father of Possibleology and Possibility Education Awareness*

# Reflection

# Your Baby Feels What

During my first pregnancy with my daughter, I went through some hurtful things. I didn't quite understand my life and why things were happening the way they were. Why was there so much hurt and pain during my pregnancy? In fact, I struggled with my emotions. My emotions were all over the place. One day sitting in my grandfather's office after school, he looked me in the eyes and said, "Daughter, be happy because the baby feels everything that you feel." From that moment, I tried my best to take control of my emotions. I didn't want my daughter to feel the hurt, the pain, the depression, the upset, and the failures, so I did whatever it took so that my baby girl wouldn't feel those negative emotions.

I remember those exact words from my grandfather during my second pregnancy. So, I had to take charge of the negative thoughts and emotions. I couldn't let certain things bother me or hurt me; I didn't want my baby boy to feel those emotions. The moments that I wanted to let my emotions control me, I instantly thought about my son. As a mother living in a negatively charged world, I didn't want my babies to suffer before they arrived. I'm not saying I didn't have some days where I was just over it. In both pregnancies, I experienced some hurt that I never thought I would, but I couldn't stay down for the sake of my babies.

From mother to mother, protect your seeds by understanding your baby feels what you feel. You are in control of how you use your emotions to respond to situations. Protect your environment; if it costs you your peace, then it's not good for your seed. Dismiss any negative energy that may cause you to compromise your character, joy, happiness, or peace; your children will thank you later.

In addition, anger, rage, bitterness, and unforgiveness are also unhealthy for your pregnancy. Once again, your baby feels that. I encourage you to let all of the hurt, anger, bitterness or unforgiveness go. Your children need you, all of you. Your children need the healed you, the joyful you, the hopeful you, the whole you, and the you GOD created you to be. Challenges will arise; yes, things may hurt you, and people may walk away, but you must place your faith in GOD and know He has already worked out your situations.

GOD, here is a list of everything I need to let go of.
I release them to you right now.

Date: _____

1. _____
_____

2. _____
_____

3. _____
_____

4. _____
_____

5. _____
_____

6. _____
_____

7. _____
_____

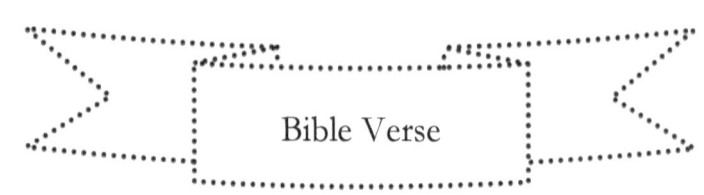

Bible Verse

"You will keep him in perfect peace, whose mind is stayed on You, because he trusts in You."

~Isaiah 26:3 (ESV)

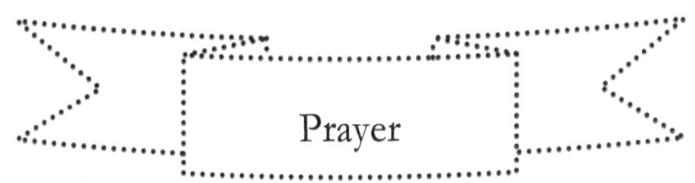

# Prayer

Heavenly Father, thank you for being my source in the times where I didn't know what to do. Thank you for being my strength in my times of weakness. Daddy, thank you for not abandoning me. For your word says you will not forsake the work of your hands, and I am the work of your hands. I let go of any and everything that would cause me to be a hindrance to becoming the mother and daughter you created me to be. I let go of anything that does not bring joy and add to the peace in my life. I am yours, and so are my children. In Jesus' name, Amen.

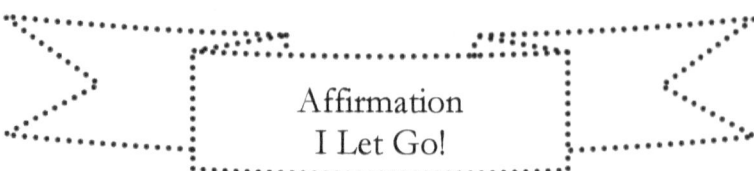

**Affirmation
I Let Go!**

I let go of the hurt.

I let go of the pain.

I let go of the failure.

I let go of the rejection.

I let go of the fear.

I let go of the worry.

I let go of the doubt.

I let go of anything and everything that does not make me a better mother.

# Reflection

## His Love Makes Me Beautiful!

*"For you formed my inward parts; you knitted me together in my mother's womb. I praise you, for I am fearfully and wonderfully made. Wonderful are your works; my soul knows it very well" (Ps. 139:13–14). ESV*

"I'm not pretty," "I'm fat," "My body is not the same," and "I don't like myself anymore" are some of the words women have said to themselves during their pregnancy. Our bodies go through so many physical changes within those nine months that women often dislike their bodies. These changes sometimes lead to women developing low self-esteem. But during these times, we can always turn to the Word of GOD. GOD'S Word said that "We are fearfully and wonderfully made. Wonderful are Your works, and since we are the workmanship of His Hands, GOD has made everything beautiful concerning His daughters during the physical changes that occur on the journey of motherhood.

Our value in Christ doesn't change because our figure or shape changes. Our value is fixated on the price Jesus paid on the cross. So, yes, it is easy to get distracted by self-loathing and who we are on this journey. It is imperative that we cast down those vain thoughts and speak GOD'S truth concerning who we are. My pastor once said, "We become what we speak," and to remember your seed hears what you are saying. What we speak determines the altitude of our life. In other words, our life is guided by the words that we release. If we speak positively, our life will go far, and if we speak negatively, our life will go the opposite direction.

If these negative thoughts about your self-image are not challenged, they eventually will turn into self-hate, even depression. You are the apple of GOD'S eye! (Zechariah 2:8). You are beautiful. You are GOD'S work of art. You are created in His image. You are GOD'S daughter. GOD takes delight in you.

On this journey of motherhood, you must understand GOD'S love for you and then love yourself out of HIS love. Hence, if you are ignorant concerning GOD'S love for you, you cannot love yourself correctly. This means you can only love yourself, your child, and others to the extent that you are aware of GOD's love for you (Dr. Oscar J. Nelson Dowdell-Underwood).

Love yourself out of your awareness of Daddy GOD'S love for you. Love all of you. Love the changes that come with pregnancy. Love the changes that come with motherhood. Love the good and the bad, and whatever you struggle to love, ask GOD to show more of His love evident in your life so that you can love yourself. Make it a habit to rehearse and affirm GOD'S Truth about you. His Truth is His Word. You are a child of GOD; stand on GOD'S Truth and believe His promises.

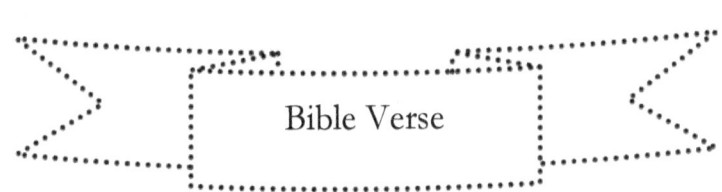
Bible Verse

*"Charm is deceitful, and beauty is vain, but a woman who fears the LORD is to be praised"*
*Prov. 31:30*

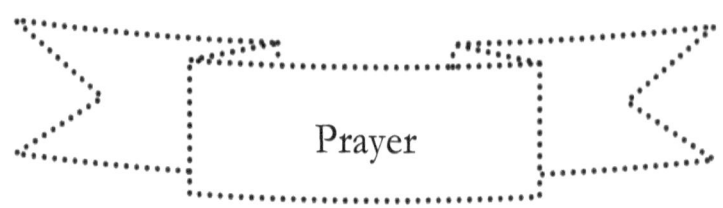

## Prayer

Dear, Heavenly Father.

Daddy, thank you for creating me. Thank you that everything concerning me, inside and out, is made beautiful. You created me beautiful. No matter how I feel, I will trust you and your Word concerning me. I am your masterpiece that is perfectly knitted together. I thank you for loving me and when I begin to doubt my love for myself, remind me of your love for me. In Jesus' name, Amen.

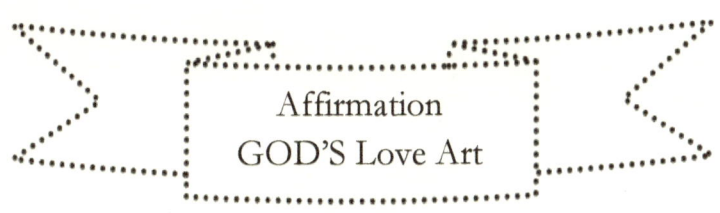

## Affirmation
## GOD'S Love Art

I am beautiful in every way possible.

Everything about me is beautiful.

I was created by GOD, and nothing He creates is ugly.

I am GOD'S piece of Art, knitted by His love.

It is out of His love that I love myself and others.

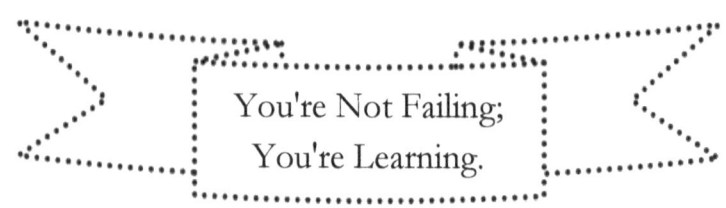

## You're Not Failing; You're Learning.

Have you ever felt like you were failing in life? Maybe failing as a wife, friend, parent, or failing in your career. I have!!! I remember talking to my grandfather, mentor, and Pastor, Dr. Oscar J. Nelson Dowdell-Underwood on the phone about what I was facing in my life at that time. I told my grandfather, I felt like I was failing as a mother, a wife, and as a teacher. He responded, "You're not failing as a wife; you're learning as a wife. You're not failing as mother; you're learning as a mother. You're not failing as a teacher; you're learning as a teacher. It was at that moment where my grandfather's words challenged me to look at my circumstances differently and view them through the lens of CHRIST. Therefore, I didn't feel nor did I see myself as a failure anymore. My grandfather caused me to challenge every limitation and lie that I placed on myself.

Whatever you're feeling or going through, I want to encourage you today with the words of my grandfather, "You're not failing; you're learning." I want to challenge your perspective concerning how you see the problems and circumstances that you're facing in your life right now. It's time to stop perceiving your mistakes or the things that you feel like you're doing wrong as failure but use them as opportunities to learn something that you never knew.

Beloved, child of GOD, it's time to ask GOD for the Grace to eliminate the thoughts of being a failure. Philippians 4:13 (NKJV) says, " I can do all things through CHRIST who strengthens me." The Bible also says, "We are more than conquerors (Romans 8:37)." Therefore, Christ lives in you and His strength makes you more than a conqueror. There's nothing in life that can stop you or cause you to fail. Failure is not a final destination when CHRIST'S Holy Ghost power dwells in you.

So, when you feel like you've missed the mark, don't immediately see yourself as a failure, but look for opportunities to grow and learn. My grandfather taught me that you grow into the person that GOD created you to be, and you can only grow to the degree of knowledge and revelation you receive. You can't become, nor can you make the impact that GOD desires for you to make, if you are holding on to a dead weight, such as failure. GOD allows failure to promote us, not to destroy us.

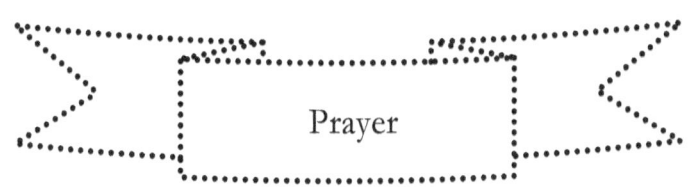

## Prayer

Daddy,

    I am so glad that I am loved by you. It is your love that gives me the strength to rise above this depression. It does not matter what others think or say about me. I am your child. When I am sad, you are my comforter. When I am broken, you are my healer. When I am weak, you are my strength. When I am confused, you are my truth. When I am down, you are the lifter of my head. GOD, in you, I am made whole and alive. In Jesus' name. Amen.

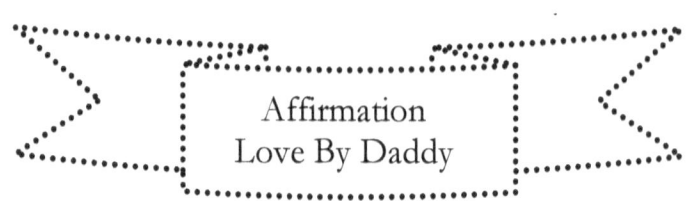

## Affirmation
## Love By Daddy

I am loved by my daddy, GOD.

When I am down, He lifts me up.

When I cry, He dries my tears.

When it is dark in my life, He is my bright and morning star.

When I am weak, I am strong in Him.

There is nothing like being loved by GOD.

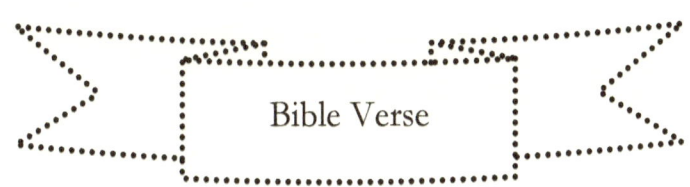

Bible Verse

The LORD is a refuge for the oppressed, a stronghold in times of trouble.

~ Psalms 9:9

# Reflection

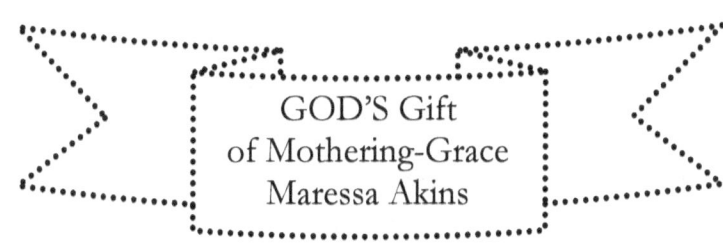

# GOD'S Gift of Mothering-Grace
## Maressa Akins

*"For you created my inmost being; you knit me together in my mother's womb. I praise you because I am fearfully and wonderfully made; your works are wonderful, I know that full well."* -Psalm 139:13-14

Babies are one of God's most precious gifts. Upon conception, a woman's body will spend three-fourths of a year going through a change that is nothing short of miraculous. Although there may be times when the mommy-to-be feels exhausted, unappreciated, and simply unlike herself, she should find solace in knowing that the DNA that has formed in her womb is that of no one else that has ever set foot on this earth. Therefore, she is carrying a gift that only God can give.

Do you remember the first time you heard your baby's heartbeat or saw your baby's face on an ultrasound screen? I do. It's usually in those moments when everything shifts into perspective. It is also those moments that will help you get through the tough and overwhelming moments that life will bring during your time of pregnancy. In fact, the reality of caring for such an innocent and helpless little person can be scary for some who worry about financial support or how to provide a safe and stable home. However, it is important to keep in mind that God will not give a vision without provision. So, I encourage you to put your trust in the Lord because He will provide for all of your needs, even before you know of their existence.

As a "very" pregnant, divorced, African-American woman and mother of a 4-year-old, I can testify to the fact that God has been one hundred percent faithful to the provision of my needs, far beyond anything that I could ask of a man.

At the beginning of the pandemic (March 2020), I was between jobs and had experienced a devastating breakup with my (ex-)fiance. So, I decided to return to school to complete my Bachelor's Degree in Psychology. By the summer, I had met a Nigerian man who was temporarily in the U.S. as he strived to pursue his Ph.D. We experienced a short courtship because we knew that he was scheduled to return home within a few months of our meeting. However, it was during that time that I became pregnant. We were both shocked!

By December, he returned home to Nigeria, unable to return to the U.S. until further notice because of his student visa. Meanwhile, here I remained with a toddler, a baby on the way, and no fathers in sight. I experienced a wide range of emotions, from resentment to loneliness and even depression. So, I actively sought-after peace, forgiveness, and understanding from God, all of which He fulfilled. And even though I have been out of work for several months due to the pandemic, God has supplied me with an over-abundance of financial support ("...pressed down, shaken together and running over"). Now, our loving families and I are just a couple of weeks away from meeting another one of God's precious gifts, the Nigerian princess. So, put your trust in God and have hope in the future because He has already declared that your latter will be greater than your former.

Whether this is your first or fourth pregnancy, do not be afraid but have hope. You were built for this. Whether you are married or single, do not feel overwhelmed, but have hope. You were built for this. Whether your pregnancy was "planned" or "unplanned,"; do not be anxious, but have hope. You were built for this. Whether God purposed you to bear life during a worldwide pandemic or if you experience a loss, do not be depressed but have hope. You were built for this.

*"Yet you brought me out of the womb; you made me trust in you even at my mother's breast. From birth I was cast*

*upon you; from my mother's womb you have been my God."* –
Psalm 22:9-10

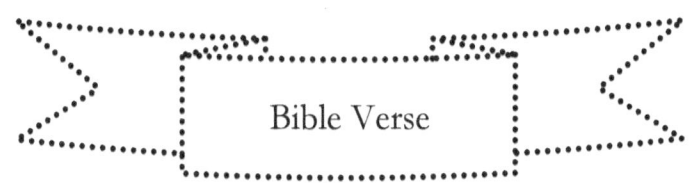
Bible Verse

You know that such testing of your faith produces endurance. Endure until your testing is over. Then you will be mature and complete, and you won't need anything.

~ James 1:4-5 (GWT)

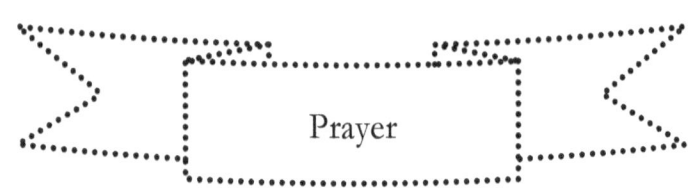

## Prayer

Jehovah Jireh, My Provider, the one who takes care of all my needs. Thank you, daddy, that I don't have to worry or question if you are going to provide for me. Your Word says you will. So, I don't have to worry when I'm at my lowest or my highest. I stand on and rehearse your Word, for it will surely come to pass. In Jesus' name, Amen.

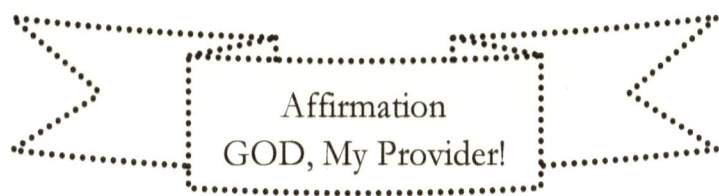

## Affirmation
## GOD, My Provider!

I will not worry

I will not stress

I will not beg

All my needs are met in Jesus Christ

Because GOD is my provider

# Reflection

## Time Heals All Wounds
### Kecia Williams

I never thought, at the age of 26, that I would have to make one of the hardest decisions of my life and how the outcome would play out in the lives of so many others. I realized that the decision I was about to make would affect the lives of my children forever. I was scared to face such a big life-changing decision by myself; however, I was alone and had no choice.

I was 26 and six months pregnant when I decided to give my son, that I was carrying, up for adoption. I didn't even know how to cope with what I had just decided and didn't really have any family support to help me with this decision.

I went through this amazing adoption agency that was patient, kind, and never forced me to make any decisions that I wasn't comfortable making or unsure about. I didn't take making this decision lightly. When I got pregnant with my son, I was already taking care of four kids and was living with a family member in a one-bedroom apartment.

"Why would I get pregnant again," many asked. It was not like many people thought: I looked for love in all of the wrong places. I was in a very dark place in my life and wasn't always making the best decisions, including having unprotected sex. So, when I found out that I was pregnant with baby number five, the shock alone left me in doubt for the first two months. All the way until I found the family to adopt him, I weighed out all my options at that time, and adoption was the best for me. This does not mean it wasn't a hard decision to make.

Fast forward, after I place my son with his wonderful family, it was not until a few months later that I fell into a terrible depression, and it wasn't from guilt. It was from a lot of negativity I received, mostly from family members. It came to a point where I felt worthless, and I felt like I shouldn't be able to be a mother to my children. I felt lower than low, and I battled with that for years until I started attending Destiny Dome Embassy at Cathedral of Praise, and experienced GOD'S Love through the Word brought forth by Dr. Nelson Dowdell-Underwood. I learned that I am not others' opinions of me.

In closing, I want to encourage anyone that may have or may be thinking about adoption; please don't let others make you feel like you're less than or adoption is a bad thing. Do your own research and make the decision that is best for you and your family. My adoption turned out to be a GOD Connection. But this is to be continued until my next story. Stay tuned. May God Bless anyone that reads this, and may you find peace. "Be Strong, and let your heart take courage, all you who wait on the Lord! Psalm 31:240 (ESV)"

Bible Verse

It is dangerous to be concerned with what others think of you, but if you trust the Lord, you are safe.

~ Proverbs 29:25 (GNT)

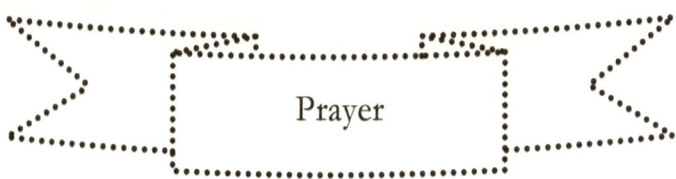

## Prayer

Father GOD!

I thank you that I don't have to rely on people's opinions. All I need to rely on is Your Word and Your Promises concerning me. I am not who people say I am. I am who You created me to be. GOD, I ask for the Grace to not worry about people's opinions about me. I must do what is best for my family and me, and Your Word will guide my decisions. Daddy, thank you for loving me and seeing the best in me. In Jesus' Name, Amen!

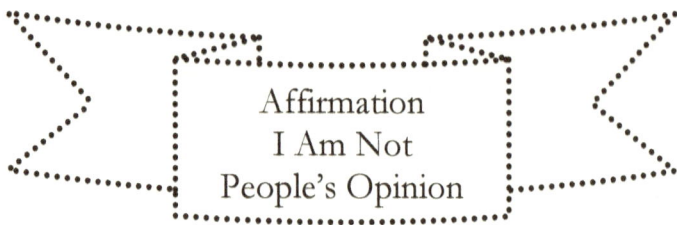

## Affirmation
## I Am Not People's Opinion

I Am Not People's Opinions.

I am who GOD says I am!

I am GOD'S Daughter!

I am a Child of GOD!

I am not my mistakes!

I am not my failures!

I am made new in Christ!

I am a chosen and holy vessel of GOD!

I am who GOD says I am.

# Reflection

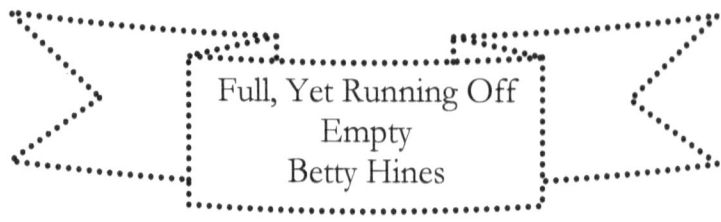

## Full, Yet Running Off Empty
### Betty Hines

When I was asked to contribute a story concerning my pregnancy, I laughed. Seriously? Sometimes, we tend to lean to our own understanding before we allow the Holy Spirit to bring clarity to the matter at hand.

A few days later, as I was listening to the Book of Psalms on my NKJV Audio Bible, Psalm 127:3-4 really caught my attention. I believe it was because I was struggling with what to write concerning being pregnant.

Psalm 127:3-4 NKJV says,

**"Behold, children are a heritage from the Lord; the fruit of the womb *is* a reward. Like arrows in the hand of a warrior, so *are* the children of one's youth."**

Now, I will introduce myself. My name is Betty. I am 68 years young. Yes, "years young!" GOD blessed me with three "arrows." And I was/am like a "warrior" where my heritage (inheritance) from the Lord is concerned. I was a single mother at the age of 17, with my firstborn.

When I had my second child, I was 19 and married. Drum roll, at the age of 21, I had my third "arrow" and was once again a single mother, not of one "arrow" but now, three! My firstborn went home to be with the Lord at the age of 24. Perhaps, I will share more details of that experience in another testimony.

This story is not just to encourage single women but all women concerning pregnancy. As you can see, I have been there on both ends – single and married.

Focus on the scripture – the Word of GOD! No matter the circumstance or situation you find yourself in concerning having been pregnant or are pregnant, know this first that **"children are a heritage (*inheritance*) from the Lord, the fruit of the womb is a reward."**

Let me be clear; the road was not easy raising three children but, it was and still is rewarding to know that GOD entrusts me with His "arrows" to nurture. In addition, GOD provided me with great support systems along the way. I now understand that He equipped me to be a mother. I would not trade it for anything because as a mother is nurturing her young, she too is being nurtured. I do not have a word that describes the feeling of a child's reaction to his/her mother's loving care, except maybe heart-throbbing.

For everyone born of God overcomes the world. This is the victory that has overcome the world, even our faith. 1 John 5:4

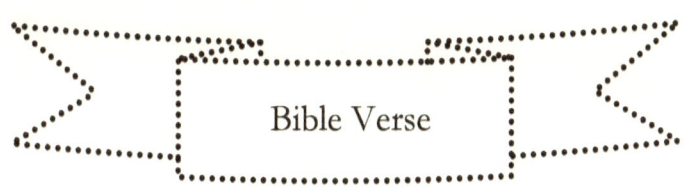

Bible Verse

"Behold, children are a heritage from the Lord, the fruit of the womb *is* a reward. Like arrows in the hand of a warrior, so *are* the children of one's youth."

~ Psalms 127:3-4 (KJV)

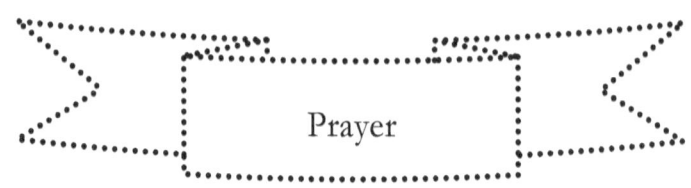

## Prayer

Dear Precious GOD,

    I thank you for being GOD, our creator. You created the heavens and the earth, the moon and the stars. Father GOD, most of all, you created your children, who you place your Spirit in. GOD, there's something special about humanity because we were the only creation made in your image. Because we are made in your image, there's nothing we can't do, including birthing, raising, and nurturing the gifts you gave us to steward on this earth as a child. Father, GOD, I ask you for strength when I feel weak as a mother. I ask for guidance when I feel lost as a parent. I ask for patience when I feel frustrated with my children. I ask for peace when I feel overwhelmed. Daddy, I know you will protect me and my children. We belong to you because we came out of you. In Jesus' Name, Amen

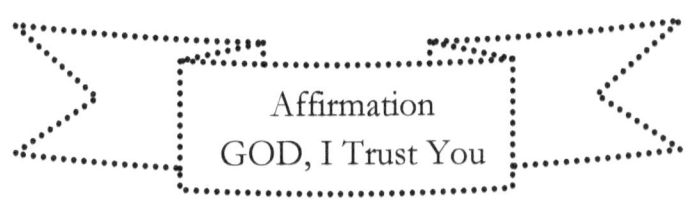

## Affirmation
## GOD, I Trust You

GOD, I Trust you.

I know my Heavenly Father will not put more on me than I can bear.

I will trust the process.

For the process will lead me to live the life I dream of for my children and myself.

## Bible Reflection

# Hope in God's Promises
## Simone Elie

Pregnancy is the anticipation of hope and an experience of the miraculous. Many times, throughout my pregnancy, I found myself, along with my husband and family, envisioning how our baby would be, what he would look like and all the ways he would change the world. This was our anticipation of hope, as we waited and expected something gracious to come from this new beginning.

When I found out that I was pregnant with my son, a range of emotions came with the news. This was my first child, and through the rush of hormones and mix of emotions, the reality was that there was also cause for concern. I am a Type 2 Diabetic with chronic high blood pressure. This automatically labeled me by doctors as high-risk- meaning I would have to be more attentive to my body and baby's activities than the average expecting mom. My husband and I recognized that our faith in God had to take precedence over fear and concern. I knew early that I would need a Word from God to carry me through the next nine months. I wanted to enjoy my pregnancy, mindfully experiencing each moment, and be in tune with my body to provide my child with the best environment.

During the first trimester, I found a devotional book that ministered to pregnant women and provided daily prayers, scriptures and medical insight on baby development and growth. The first devotion led with the scripture Jeremiah 29:11 ESV, "For I know the plans I have for you, declares the LORD, plans to prosper you and not to harm you, plans to give you hope and a future." Immediately, I received the scripture as a promise for me and my baby, and from then on, it consistently encouraged me in moments of anxiety. I can remember praying and rehearsing the Word after appointments when I was instructed to go home and count baby kicks to monitor his movements. Other times when I checked my blood glucose before measuring my insulin injections, I was comforted by His Word. I grew closer to God, understanding how to totally and completely lean on Him. Never had I been so aware of my eagerness to be in control. Even when I thought I had "cast my cares" upon the Lord, I would find myself trying to problem-solve. I accepted that I had to give everything to God and trust Him wholeheartedly. I would do my part in faith, surrender and be anchored by His promise in Jeremiah.

My husband, a prayerful, warring man of God, would welcome in the Spirit of God through praise and worship before we prayed together. In our prayers, we gave our baby back to God even before he was born. Our child was God's first and foremost, given as a gift to us. The Lord never let a prayer go unanswered, and despite diabetes and high blood pressure, I was able to deliver my son full term at 37 weeks. My baby boy was everything I could have ever hoped for. Now, almost six years later, each time Jeremiah 29:11 comes to me, I think to myself, "This is my son's scripture, his life scripture," and I thank God for His living, breathing Word.

Today, I hope that you are strengthened and compelled to hold on to the promises of God, be it revealed through scripture or the man or woman of God. Receive and rehearse each promise so that your hope and faith increase. When times look hard, feel chaotic, and you need clarity, remember what the future truly holds and what is rightfully yours.

"Let us not become weary in doing good, for at the proper, time we will reap a harvest if we do not give up. Galatians 6:9"

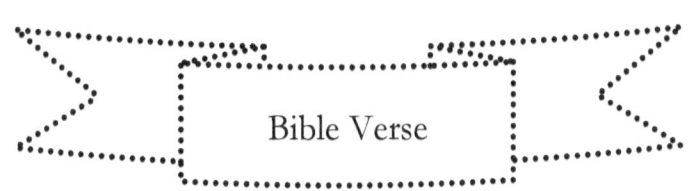

Bible Verse

"For I know the plans I have for you," declares the LORD, "plans to prosper you and not to harm you, plans to give you hope and a future."

~ Jeremiah 29:11

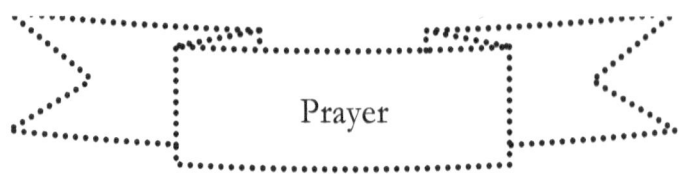

## Prayer

Heavenly Father, you are Omniscience, all-knowing. I thank you that you know the plans for my life, and those plans are not to harm me but to prosper me and do me good. The Bible is full of promises from you, GOD, and I stand on Jeremiah 29:11. All I have to do is believe and rest in your Word because you have everything concerning me and my child planned out. You know the end from the beginning, and therefore, all I know to do is trust you, GOD, and your Word. I place my pregnancy, my baby, and my future in your hands because you already have it designed out. In Jesus' Name, Amen.

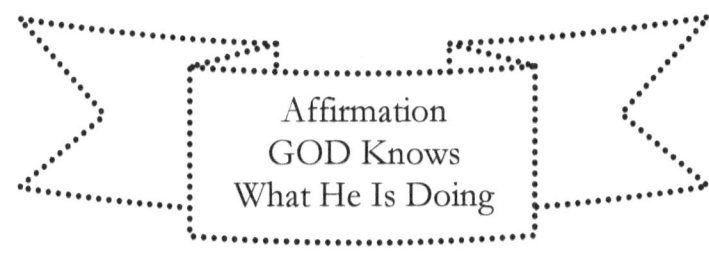

### Affirmation
### GOD Knows What He Is Doing

GOD Knows What He Is Doing.
I will trust GOD.
I do not need to worry because He has taken care of everything concerning me.
GOD will not abandon me.
I belong to GOD, and I am His Child created in His Image.
Therefore, I will trust GOD.
He knows what He is doing.
His plans are great for my future.

# Reflection

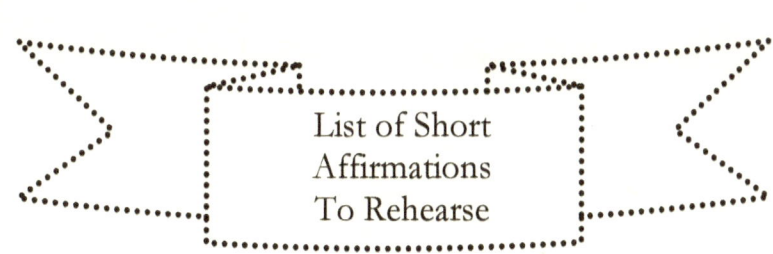

## List of Short Affirmations To Rehearse

1. I am doing an amazing job!
2. I got this!
3. I am loved!
4. My children are not a mistake!
5. My children are my hope!
6. GOD has already worked it out!
7. GOD, thank you for my children!
8. I stand on GOD Promises!
9. I believe GOD!
10. I will break generational curses! My children will not have to go through what I went through!

# My Words Have Power: My Personal Affirmations
## (Create your own affirmations)

1. _____

_____

2. _____

_____

3. _____

_____

4. _____

_____

5. _____

_____

6. _____

_____

7. _____

_____

# Bible Verses
# For The Journey

"Peace I leave with you, my peace I give to you; not as the world gives do I give to you. Let not your heart be troubled, neither let it be afraid."
— John 14:27

"Do not be anxious about anything, but in every situation, by prayer and petition, with thanksgiving, present your requests to God. And the peace of God, which transcends all understanding, will guard your hearts and your minds in Christ Jesus."
— Philippians 4:6-7

"I will both lie down in peace, and sleep; for You alone, O LORD, make me dwell in safety."
— Psalm 4:8

Give your burdens to the Lord, and he will take care of you. He will not permit the godly to slip and fall.
– Psalm 55:22

Fear not, for I am with you; be not dismayed, for I am your God; I will strengthen you, I will help you, I will uphold you with my righteous right hand.
— Isaiah 41:10 (ESV)

# Psalm 23

<sup>1</sup>The Lord is my shepherd, I lack nothing.
² He makes me lie down in green pastures,
he leads me beside quiet waters,
³ he refreshes my soul.
He guides me along the right paths
for his name's sake.
⁴ Even though I walk
through the darkest valley,[a]
I will fear no evil,
for you are with me;
your rod and your staff,
they comfort me

## Psalm 139:13-18

<sup>13</sup> For you created my inmost being;
you knit me together in my mother's womb.
<sup>14</sup> I praise you because I am fearfully and wonderfully made;
your works are wonderful,
I know that full well.
<sup>15</sup> My frame was not hidden from you
when I was made in the secret place,
when I was woven together in the depths of the earth.
<sup>16</sup> Your eyes saw my unformed body;
all the days ordained for me were written in your book
before one of them came to be.

# Bible Reflection

# Journal For Weary Days

# Journal For Weary Days

# My Story: My Journey To Motherhood

# My Story: My Journey To Motherhood

Do you have a story that you would like to encourage and empower others with?
Visit www.youcanmakeitbooks.com

# You Can Make It!!!

www.ingramcontent.com/pod-product-compliance
Lightning Source LLC
Chambersburg PA
CBHW030914080526
44589CB00010B/298